CULTIVATING
COMPASSION

CULTIVATING COMPASSION

Simple Everyday Practices for Discovering Peace of Mind and Resilience

Amy Pattee Colvin

ISBN-10: 0-9980799-0-1
ISBN-13: 978-0-9980799-0-5

Cover Design: Ida Fia Sveningsson
Editor: Nancy Pattee Malitz
Illustrator: Leslie Malitz Vukasovich

CONTENTS

ACKNOWLEDGEMENTS

Those teachers, family, friends, and students who have helped me learn about acceptance and compassion for self and others are too numerous to mention, but know that I appreciate all the lessons you've offered me along the way.

However, I want to express deep-hearted gratitude, in particular, to my long time meditation teachers, Leong Tan and Meg McLaughlin. Thank you both for your wisdom and that of Wong Loh and Kuan Yin which you have shared with us. Without your presence and insight this book would not have been written. Thank you for your kindness, humor, generosity, and inexhaustible knowledge.

INTRODUCTION

Have you ever found yourself losing sleep due to worry? Or had days when you're down in the dumps and feel like you can't shake it? Or how about times when you are just plain grouchy and snap at others while criticizing yourself? Do you ever feel lonely even though you're surrounded by people?

Stress, depression, and anxiety have been present in many modern cultures for decades. A while ago I watched Hacking Your Brain for Happiness, a 2016 TEDx Talk by Dr. James Doty, a Clinical Professor in the Department of Neurosurgery at Stanford University and the Founder/Director of the Center for Compassion and Altruism Research and Education at Stanford University School of Medicine. He mentioned that in the United States of America (USA) approximately 20% of the adult population takes prescription medication to help curb anxiety and depression. Taking into consideration self-medication with alcohol, this number goes up. As of 2016, about 50% of the adult population in the USA is using some sort of substance to help them cope with feelings of stress, unhappiness, and isolation.

Current research suggests anxiety and depression are on the rise, even with the advent of prescription medication. According to NYTimes.com in August of 2016, Google search rates for anxiety have more than doubled between 2008-2016.

As a counter-point, Doty also mentions that **cultivating compassion** has a positive effect on blood pressure, heart rate, and immune systems, as well as optimizing decision making, creativity, and sense of calm. Practicing compassion, according to a paper published in Motivation and Emotion Journal in February of 2014, decreases worry and emotional suppression.

Why does this research matter? For those of us who like to have proof of things, research validates the idea that incorporating **acceptance and compassion** into daily life **makes a difference**. Consistent incorporation of acceptance and compassion enhances your life, and in turn has an effect on the lives of others.

Rather than suggesting you sit on a cushion alone in silence, this book will help you develop habits of integrating acceptance and kindness into daily life. It supports you while you develop new positive habits. This book is for anyone who desires greater peace of mind, resilience, and is willing to enact positive change.

Self-acceptance and self-compassion is the springboard for extending acceptance and compassion to others. Imagine how your community, your state, your country, even the world would look if **everyone rose to the challenge** of being greater than stress, depression, anxiety, and judgment.

How do I know compassion meditation works? I've experienced it personally. I've spent hundreds of hours in meditation workshops and retreats over two decades. I'm personally familiar with anxiety, depression, and social isolation. I know what it is like to dabble with meditation and not see results. I know what a life-saver it was when I needed and really committed to a regular practice.

A few years ago I used to ride the bus to work. An unhealthy situation cropped up in my life that needed to change, but I spent most of my time pushing it under the rug, pretending it wasn't there. One day, as the bus drove onto a bridge, I thought, "Boy, it sure would be nice to drop into that water. It would be easy to slip in and never come up. I'd rather do that than deal with this situation." Hmmm... okay. Fleeting thought. The next day, I had the same thought, and the next day, and the next. Whoa! Way more than a fleeting thought now. I knew I wouldn't take harmful action and jump into the water. However, I could no longer deny that something within me needed to change.

I considered what tools I had that could help me. Meditation came to mind. I remembered all those insights and techniques my teachers shared with me and I thought, "Well, it's worth a try," and I started a daily meditation practice.

Sometimes it felt really peaceful. Sometimes my brain would spin, and I'd remind myself to go back to my breath and be patient. Sometimes I'd be overwhelmed by grief and despair, and cry my eyes out—but I stuck with it because I knew in the long run the difficult situation would resolve.

Sure enough, it did. Committing to a meditation practice helped me cultivate the courage to create change. It helped me remember to focus on the positive. It helped me notice when those self-critical stories came to mind, and reminded me to redirect my thought process. It helped me discover peace of mind and raise resilience.

In truth, I have to say that a **regular meditation practice completely transformed my life in a positive way**. And meditation may have a profound impact in your life as well!

Whether you're stuck in despair as I was, or if you have a generally happy life but want to work on settling your mind, being more creative and productive, or lowering your blood pressure; compassion meditation may make a difference.

Eventually I realized I wanted to share these tools and techniques for developing compassion meditation. I began facilitating courses and offering private self-compassion coaching with the intention of helping people integrate Taoist and Buddhist philosophy into daily life.

Health care providers, teachers, business professionals, engineers, millennials, baby boomers, and many others who struggle with acceptance and compassion for self and others have benefited from the ideas presented via courses and coaching. Many of those concepts are presented in this book.

Recently an elementary school teacher shared with me that she had the best teaching year of her life due to tools and techniques she learned from my course and **put into action.** As a result, she was better equipped to connect with her students and had more confidence in her work.

Another student mentioned that she maintained a "protective emotional shell" much of her life. The insights offered in my course, and now through this book, helped her loosen that shell and explore ways to reduce the need for that barrier. She said learning acceptance and compassion for self was incredibly valuable. It helped her cultivate forgiveness and boundary setting, but with compassion rather than anger or defensiveness.

I believe if you follow this book by **reading and integrating** the inspirational themes, **contemplating** the self-reflection questions, and **acting** on the informal practices, you will notice a positive change in your life.

You will find more peace within yourself. You will find your relationships with others enriched.

Having a "formal" sitting practice of 10 or more minutes a day is important. But, **integrating acceptance and compassion into daily life is critical**. Daily implementation drives positive change and creates healthy habits.

Regardless of your history with meditation practice—lots, some, none—be content with what you have done, and strive to do more. Be kind to yourself in the process of starting a new habit.

Don't be one of those people who think about starting a meditation practice but never get around to it. Or one of those people who says, "Oh, I try to meditate every day, but it just doesn't really stick."

Don't be one of those people who reads a book on meditation or compassion, puts it down, carries on just as you had been, and wonders why life is still the same. Hey, you just *read* a book on meditation right? Isn't that enough? Nope.

Take action. Now.

Read the book. Really understand and integrate the inspirational ideas, all of which emerged from decades of meditation retreats. Take time to write answers to the self-reflection questions. Put the informal practices into action.

Daily.

Have you heard the adage from neuroscience— "What fires together wires together?" How you think and how you act, every day, shapes the next day. And the next. And the next. **You have the power**

to choose how to live this life. Live it with acceptance, compassion, and harmony.

Get out of the ditch. Get on the road to positive change.

Do it. Now.

If you invest in yourself and do the work, your life will change for the better.

As you change your life, you'll inspire others. As others are touched in a positive way, they'll affect even more people. A ripple effect of acceptance and compassion will continue outward.

Changing your perspective on life changes the world. Start today. And, have fun!

PROLOGUE

In the same TEDx Talk by Dr. James Doty mentioned in the introduction, was an analogy I found quite effective. Essentially Dr. Doty suggested that we think of meditation like taking a pill, and following a prescription.

This pill and prescription reduce anxiety, stress, depression, and social isolation. Blood pressure and heart rate become lower. Creativity, productivity, and responses to life's challenges, rather than reactions, are enhanced. This solution has no negative side effects and is virtually free.

However, you have to follow the prescription instructions carefully:

1) **Take your pill**, which could be anything (an almond, an M&M, a cookie, a strawberry, whatever you prefer).

2) Then **sit quietly** for 10-15 minutes and focus your attention on your breathing, while thinking kind thoughts for yourself and others.

The **only way the pill will work is to follow this prescription exactly.** Don't take the pill then immediately run off to do something else. You must be still, breathe deeply, let your body and mind relax, and think kind thoughts.

Sitting quietly with yourself is the foundation, the essence, of a meditation practice. An excellent way to cultivate acceptance and compassion for self and others is through creating a consistent compassion meditation practice, blending a bit of sitting still with expressing intentional actions out in the world.

Compassion combines:

1) **Awareness**—acknowledging distress in yourself or others;

2) **Empathy**—being emotionally moved by this distress;

3) **Action**—making some sort of response, which could involve some sort of physical action, or it could be as subtle as mentally/intentionally sending someone well wishes.

Cultivating acceptance and compassion helps you settle your mind, befriend your inner critic, embrace your vulnerability, and reframe your comparisons to others.

The simple act of sitting quietly for a few minutes a day, breathing gently but deeply, and focusing on acceptance and compassion can transform your perspective.

Cultivating acceptance and compassion helps you embrace and move through anxiety, self-criticism, and depression. You become grounded in wellbeing. You discover peace of mind and resilience.

Once you achieve a stable platform of acceptance and compassion for yourself, you naturally reflect that healthy state-of-being outward. You become greater than an individual, lost in social isolation. You engage with your community and extend your acceptance and compassion to others.

It is **not hard work**. I'm not suggesting you sit in total stillness for 45 minutes staring at the wall, although you could. You certainly don't need to wear a white robe, burn candles and incense, and start chanting, although that would be fine if you enjoy it. Change arises from willingness to do the work.

You must have patience, and you must put these ideas and perspectives into action daily.

It will be uncomfortable at times. I'm not going to try to fool you about that. But don't give up. Stick with it every day, and you will notice positive change. When you notice resistance, lean into it. Embrace it. Be willing to grow from it. "Fake it 'til you make it" if you have to.

Learn to and practice embracing your thoughts, emotions, and places of resistance. Get closer, take a look, experience the feelings, and move with and through the challenging times. Suppressing and denying those difficult bits will keep you stuck in the same ditch.

A research article titled How Habits are Formed, published in 2010 in the **European Journal of Social Psychology,** suggests that it takes an average of 66 days to form a new habit. 66 days to really change your outlook.

Use this book to support you as you grow.

66 Inspirations

66 Self-reflection questions

66 Informal practices

You might spend as little as 5 minutes a day. You might sit with ideas for an hour or two. Either way, **every day, take action.** Every day, work toward positive change. You will see the results.

And, don't do it alone.

Share this book with an accountability partner, and work through it together.

Engage your family; share this book with your children or parents, and check in with each other daily or weekly to see how things are going. Find a colleague at work. Get your entire team on board, and make it a 66-day challenge. Give a copy of this book to your spouse, partner, or best friend, and work through each day together. Support each other through challenges and celebrate successes.

Read the book. Take time to **understand and integrate** the inspirational ideas. Absorb the supporting context. Perhaps even think of similar examples from your own life.

Grab a notebook and **write** answers to the self-reflection questions, or write your answers in this book! Use this self-reflection as an opportunity to journal. The act of writing helps you to **commit** to this process of change.

Act. Put the informal practices into action. None of them take much time. But they will have a positive effect if you do them **daily.**

I really believe there is no wrong way to meditate. Find yourself; find peace within yourself; extend it to others.

All you have to do is start today with Day One. Then tomorrow contemplate and act on Day Two.

Each day offers new insights on how to change your perspective and cultivate acceptance and compassion for yourself and others. Be the change you want to see in the world.

After you've gone through the 66 days once, start over again. Or just flip it open to a page that suits you. Make it your own. Find a way that works for you, but be sure to take action daily. And, have fun!

FINDING THE FRIEND IN YOU

Day 1: Getting Started

There is no wrong way to meditate.
Find yourself, find peace within yourself,
extend it to others.

Are you ready? The next 66 days will be life-changing—if you **take action**. Don't worry about whether or not you're doing anything right or wrong. Don't over-think what you're doing. This book is for you, where you are **right now.**

Maybe you'll pick this book up again at a different time in life and your responses to the ideas, questions, and actions will be different. That is a joyful thing. It means you're evolving.

Meditation and mindfulness may take many forms; sitting in stillness, walking, yoga, listening to music, listening to others with an open heart. But you must **choose** to take **action in** order to experience the benefits.

Self-Reflection:
Why have I picked up this book at this time in my life? What has brought me here, at this moment? What do I hope to learn about myself? How will this affect others?

Informal Practice:

Today, at random moments, I will pay attention to my breath. I don't need to change it or do anything with it—I will simply notice it. I will observe if it is slow or fast, deep or shallow. I'll simply become more aware of this automatic action and appreciate that it keeps me alive.

Day 2: Connecting with Intention
"I want to be a better person
and I will work on that."
This is the best gift you can give yourself.

Intention is a key component of motivation. It is easy to make intention big and overwhelming, and yet it can be so simple. "I want to be a better person and I will work on that."

One breath at a time. One hour at a time. One conversation or task at a time.

If you take action and follow your intention to cultivate a compassion meditation practice, you may notice these physical benefits:

- Lower blood pressure and heart rate
- Decreased tension related pain
- Improved mood and behavior
- Strengthened immune system
- Enhanced energy level and sense of vitality

Remind yourself regularly that your intention, in whatever way is meaningful for you, is to become a better person. Use the tools and techniques offered in this book to support you in this process.

Self-Reflection:

Why am I interested in cultivating acceptance and compassion for myself and others?

Informal Practice:

Today I will experiment with breathing deeply. I will inhale, all the way into my belly, for a count of four. I will gently hold my breath for a count of four. I will exhale fully for a count of four. I will gently hold the exhale for a count of four. Then I will repeat that process a few times.

Day 3: Appreciating Yourself
"I am a good person"
is the only affirmation you need.

One benefit of settling your mind, being aware in the moment, and connecting with your inner wisdom is developing the courage to be comfortable in your own skin. This ease with your essential nature leads to deeper self-appreciation.

Can you look at yourself in the mirror, at any moment, with kindness and tenderness and say, "I am a good person," and really believe it? Try it out and see what happens.

If you notice any resistance, simply acknowledge it and don't over-analyze it. As you practice mindfulness or meditation daily, softening resistance becomes easier. Your ability to fully embrace, at all times, begins to blossom.

Learning to accept yourself in all circumstances is a skill that takes practice, courage, and diligence.

Self-Reflection:

What concerns or challenges arise when I consider cultivating compassion for myself and others?

Informal Practice:

Today I will look into a mirror and internally say, "I am a good person." I will notice what my body feels like when saying this to and for myself. If I notice resistance, I will take a few deep breaths, and try again later.

Day 4: At Home in Your Own Skin

If you know yourself, you will never be lost.
You are not lost if you are here.
If you are here then you are home.

In order to extend yourself in a helpful or compassionate way to others, you need a solid foundation of self-compassion.

One way to build a solid foundation of self-appreciation, self-acceptance, and self-compassion is through meditation or mindfulness. When your mind begins to settle, you have a better opportunity to see all of your thoughts and feelings. Sometimes you like what you see. Sometimes you'd rather not take a look. However, it is important to observe and embrace those challenging areas.

As you become at home in your own skin, and as you connect with your breath and inner wisdom, you may notice these mental benefits:

- Reduced anxiety and depression
- Improved creativity and productivity
- Freedom from unhealthy habits
- Enhanced emotional stability
- More control over your thoughts
- Greater present-moment awareness
- More insightful intuition

Self-Reflection:

If anything were possible, what would my life really look like?

Informal Practice:

Today I will use awareness of my breath as a way to connect to the present moment. When I am aware of the present moment, I will contemplate being at home in my own skin and strive to find peace there.

Day 5: Your Own Best Friend

Always find the friend in you.
It will constantly be loyal.

Often, when contemplating compassion, directing compassion elsewhere takes precedence. When we think of being kind, we think of others first. However, ensuring that you are kind and compassionate toward yourself is critical to extending compassion to others sustainably.

Meditation, by its nature of turning inward with intentional focus, nourishes you from within and calms you when you feel overwhelmed, unstable, or emotionally shut down.

As you deepen your meditation practice, you become better able to regulate your feelings as they arise. This ability to manage your emotions helps you recover more quickly from psychological challenges. You become more resilient.

Being more fully present and less scattered helps reduce mental chaos, and in turn minimizes occasional feelings of being overwhelmed.

As you continue with your meditation practice, you become more comfortable in your own skin. You rely on your inner wisdom, and your inner light to help you become your own best friend.

Self-Reflection:

What qualities in myself do I value most?
Examples might be: Adventure, Authenticity, Commitment, Courage, Curiosity, Efficiency, Generosity, Honesty, Humility, Integrity, Leadership, Loyalty, Optimism, and Willingness—to name a few.

Informal Practice:

Today I will move through my day taking action in ways that reflect at least one quality I value.

Day 6: Living Authentically

It is easy to be someone else.
It is very hard to be yourself.

Do you find that you sometimes value other's opinions of you or your actions more than you value your own?

If so, you're not alone. Thinking that way is human. However, you can change that pattern to one where you live with more authenticity. Meditation helps support this change.

As you meditate you connect with your inner wisdom. You examine all of the ideas inside your heart and mind. Choose to explore emotions and thoughts, rather than suppressing or avoiding them. When you do, you live each moment with courage, resilience, and grace.

Creating a way to enjoy meditation is important. Try not to turn meditation into one more task on your to-do list. Consider meditation as an opportunity rather than an obligation.

Meditation allows your mind to relax and be quiet in the midst of an otherwise busy day. It creates an opening for you to do something seemingly simple which, in turn, profoundly affects your physical and mental health.

Above all, remember that some days you'll find motivation to meditate will come easily, and other days motivation will be difficult to find. Try not to be hard on yourself during the unmotivated days. Do your best; even if that means simply taking a few deep breaths with a dropped gaze a few times a day.

Self-Reflection:

If anything were possible, how would I like to develop as a human being?

Informal Practice:

Today I will strive toward making decisions based on what I believe to be right rather than on what I think others might believe is right.

Day 7: Free from Self-Judgment
Do not compare yourself to others.
Know you are enough.

We all do it at one time or another—we see someone else and wish we had their attributes, their "stuff," their social position, or their skills. Ultimately all of these comparisons are external-facing, and crop up when we're not feeling 100% content with ourselves. These thoughts arise when we are in moments of self-judgment.

When you are truly content with yourself, you release comparisons. You accept yourself as you are, and you accept others as they are without a need to hold both side by side.

You are unique. Embrace that awareness. Focus on your own successes. Compete less, and appreciate others more.

Releasing comparisons may bring up resistance. Simply acknowledge the resistance, melt into it, and know that you're human. With practice, detachment from comparison will become second nature.

Self-Reflection:

What do I really want to offer the world?

Informal Practice:

Today I will let go of comparing myself to others. If I catch myself in the act of comparison, I will gently but firmly remind myself that I am enough.

Day 8: Cherishing Self

Cherishing yourself means extending your heart to yourself with respect and honor.

A wonderful parable, whose original author is unknown, goes something like this:

An elderly abbot and a few elderly monks lived in a remote monastery. They'd lived together for years and began to take each other for granted, rarely extending respect to each other or themselves.

One day an old rabbi came to visit and the abbot asked if he had advice on how to bring life back into his dying order. The rabbi sadly said that he had no advice. He did say, however, that one among the monastery was the Messiah.

Later the monks asked about the conversation, and the abbot replied, "He didn't have advice. But, he did say something very strange—he said that one among us is the Messiah."

For days they mulled this over, wondering who might be the Messiah. Ultimately they began to respect and cherish each other more than they had in years, with the thought that one among them truly was the Messiah. They also began to respect and cherish themselves as well.

Subsequently a few visitors came to meditate in the small chapel. They noticed and took comfort from the aura of respect found at the monastery. They began to bring friends, who brought more friends. Eventually a few of the young ones asked if they might stay and become monks. The order began to thrive once again.

Self-Reflection:

If I were talking to my best friend, how would I describe myself while using the language of honor and self-respect?

Informal Practice:

Today I will show myself and others extraordinary respect.

Day 9: Believe in Yourself

*Have a strong belief in you,
because everything in your life
begins and ends with you.*

No one else is living your life. How you move through your days, weeks, months, and years is up to you.

You have a choice in what you're doing and how you're treating yourself in any given moment.

Be kind to yourself. Cherish yourself. Make the commitment to grow every day and become even better. Live each day well and fully.

Be patient with yourself when you err. Pick yourself up. Reframe your outlook. Begin again. These actions take courage. Repetition builds resilience.

Take responsibility for your behavior and be the best person you can be in any moment. The quality of your life is up to you.

Self-Reflection:

What prevents me from being self-compassionate?
What supports me in being self-compassionate?

Informal Practice:

Today I will notice moments when I am being self-critical, and I will turn that around into treating myself with compassion.

Day 10: Mental Choices

Don't let your mind run wild.
Find the friend in your mind, not the enemy.

An old Chinese saying goes something like this, "In the eye of the Buddha is a dragon. In the eye of a dragon is the Buddha." It highlights the duality of nature. It reflects the duality with us. Following this idea of duality, we all have a big-self within us, and we have a little-self.

The big-self is the kind, gracious, generous self that helps us make excellent decisions. It expresses kindness, is optimistic, and often knows just the right thing to say in the right moment.

The little-self is the snarky-self that says mean things, is selfish, and contributes to less-than-optimal decisions. It expresses doubt, is pessimistic, and is that little critical voice inside our head that sometimes takes charge.

The best way to work with this little-self is to acknowledge it, befriend it, and listen to what it is really trying to say. Often that little-self pipes up because it is sad, lonely, bored, or worried.

Rather than suppress or deny this inner critic, hold out your hand. Let that little-self know you're listening. Ask it what it really needs. Soothe its concern. Give it a hug and some crayons or cocoa. Then ask the little-self to sit quietly next to you as you move on with your day. Often that is enough to settle it down and calm the wildness of mind.

Self-Reflection:

What techniques do I currently use to deal with my inner critic, my little-self? How might things be different if I were willing to acknowledge and befriend my little-self, listen to it, and invite it to sit quietly by rather than ruling my day?

Informal Practice:

Today I will be more aware of negative self-talk. I will consider that critical voice as my little-self, and I will listen to what it is really trying to say. Then I will l gently but firmly let it know it needs to settle down and let me move on with my day.

Day 11: No More Complaining

***Complaining and finding fault is easy.
Try not to do that.***

Have you ever done something twenty times well but remember the one time you erred? We all have. It is part of being human.

One way to move out of this cycle is through taking responsibility. Taking responsibility means not blaming anyone or anything for a given situation. This includes blaming yourself. If an obstacle or complication arises, acknowledge it and work toward a solution.

Problems may be opportunities in disguise. Adopting this mindset allows us to take less-than-stellar moments and transform them into greater good. Rather than complain about a past event, look for ways to prevent the future challenges.

Self-Reflection:

What benefit do I gain from finding faults in myself? How might I, and everyone with whom I interact, be better served if I fully accept myself instead?

Informal Practice:

Today, if I notice I am complaining about myself, someone else, or anything at all, I will gently stop the complaints. I will look for the good things, not the faults. I will seek opportunities in events that appear to be challenges.

SELF-ACCEPTANCE
&
SELF-COMPASSION

Day 12: Hugging Your Inner Critic

In your heart know you are enough.
Be willing to grow and become even better.

How often does your inner critic, your little-self, suggest that you aren't enough? For some people it happens quite often. So, how do you get that voice to subside? Befriending your little-self is an effective tool. It takes work, diligence, and practice but it can be done.

Recall a time that your little-self was criticizing you. Try to remember the feelings you felt as you were berated by your little-self. Try to sense the underlying feelings behind your inner critic's words.

What was the little-self really trying to convey? Was it worried, lonely, bored, mad, or sad? Inevitably your inner critic talks to you because it has some sort of unmet need.

See if you can figure out your little-self's need in the instance you imagined. Then imagine that inner critic as a small child. If a child came to you expressing fear, loneliness, boredom, anger, and sadness, wouldn't you do what you could to help ease that child's discomfort? Wouldn't you be tender, kind, and patient? Try treating your inner critic in this way and see what happens.

Notice your inner critic with a bit of detachment. Try to understand what is really being said. Once you've listened to the little-self, and comforted it, use what it is telling you as an opportunity for growth. Remind yourself, regardless of what the little-self says, that you are enough. Kindly encourage yourself to grow, and become even better.

Self-Reflection:

When I am being self-critical or self-judgmental what are the consequences of being hard on myself? How does it feel in my body? Do I find it motivates me or discourages me?

Informal Practice:

At the end of the day I will list three things I did well. I will set an intention to recognize I am enough. I will create a positive wish to grow and become even better.

Day 13: Stop Running

If you run away from yourself,
you will always be running.
Be willing to sit with yourself.

In this device-and-stress-filled world distractions are ever-present. Scheduling distraction-free time is sometimes necessary in order to experience present-moment awareness. Being distraction-free creates an opportunity to sit with yourself, which at times can be amazingly difficult.

I like to hike with my pup, Lily. We go early to enjoy the forest on our own. I revel in seeing the trees and ferns. I love listening to the birds and the squirrels. I generally have a calm and peaceful mind.

I typically don't solve problems, make up stories about other people, or fantasize about how things could be different. I simply walk in the woods, engage with the present moment, and connect with my breath and my body.

One day we came across people—some on their own, some hiking and chatting in small groups. One listened to earbuds, but gave me a big smile as she passed by. One pecked at her cell phone, seemingly unaware of the nature around her or her hiking companion.

How do you generally choose to connect with nature? On your own? With friends? Listening to earbuds rather than sounds of nature? Pecking away at your phone? Solving problems with a busy mind?

Perhaps they all have their place, but whether you walk in the woods, sit on a cushion, or pull weeds, remember the value of quieting your mind.

Self-Reflection:

What resistance emerges when sitting quietly with myself? How do I engage with and move through that resistance? What do I need (location, time, and/or mindset) to be willing to sit with myself?

Informal Practice:

Today I will find time to be free from distraction. I will connect with myself by spending time in nature or quietude. I will spend time sitting with myself, even if it feels uncomfortable.

Day 14: The Power of Sitting with Yourself

Sitting with yourself allows you to see the truth of who you really are. It is not easy, but it is invaluable. More good comes from this simple action than you realize.

Filling time with distractions helps us avoid looking at what is deep down inside our hearts and minds.

Imagine going snorkeling. You've found a lovely spot where you can walk into the water from the beach. Beautiful fish surround you. Paddling along, you swim around a rocky point. The next thing you know, the water becomes deeper, darker. You know bigger fish are down there, maybe even sharks!

One choice is to swim right back to the shallow water avoiding what might be in the deeper, darker water. A different choice is to face that little voice of discomfort, and stick with the deeper water.

You're greeted by turtles, not sharks. Maybe someday there would be a shark, but not today. Today you see turtles.

However, if you hadn't been willing to swim with the discomfort of the unknown, you may not have seen those turtles. Perhaps you'd always be fearful of sharks.

Sitting with yourself is similar. Sometimes you are afraid of the pain, sadness, stress, anxiety, or anger that may reside within you. But it is important to look at those feelings, to swim with those feelings, to sit with those feelings.

By sitting with yourself you uncover all aspects of self. From there you create long-term lasting change. Resilience is the ability to recognize your fears and continue forward anyway. Personal growth arises from this process.

Self-Reflection:

Do I ever avoid sitting in stillness (meditation) because I am afraid of what I might find inside? What good things might arise if I chose to sit with myself?

Informal Practice:

Today I will give myself an internal hug. I will listen with patience to whatever criticisms the little-self brings up. I will not be afraid to look at the darker corners of my mind and heart. I will courageously embrace all of who I am.

Day 15: Accepting What Is

Acceptance leads to change. Change should be for the better. You control you.

Have you ever noticed at times of physical pain, if you resist the pain it sometimes feels worse; but if you breathe into it and try to relax, it doesn't hurt so much?

Your mental and emotional discomfort reacts the same way. If you find yourself distressed, try relaxing into the distress. Embrace it. Let it wash over and through you. You'll find the difficulty passes much faster.

Regular meditation practice helps you accept events as they are and lean into difficulty.

Research shows that people who practice mindfulness and meditation often become happier. This doesn't mean their lives automatically get better. They don't necessarily stop getting sick or stop experiencing distress or challenges, or losing their jobs. They lead normal lives, like all of us do. However, the quality of their mindset and their ability to be happy in the face of difficult circumstances is more resilient.

Meditation helps you shift and change your attitude. It helps you find a way of living in balance instead of being at the mercy of the ups and downs of life. Meditation helps you cultivate peace of mind.

You really do have choice in how to engage with the challenges of your life. You can choose to ignore, suppress, deny, or get stuck in them. Or, you can choose to embrace them, melt into them, and move through them.

Self-Reflection:

How often do I remember I have choice in what I am thinking, and then act from positive choices? If I'm not making positive choices regularly, what stands in my way?

Informal Practice:

Today I will practice acceptance. Today I will accept people, situations, circumstances, and events as they occur. My acceptance is total and complete. I accept things as they are this moment, not as I wish they were.

Day 16: Letting Go of Attachment

Detachment from expectations leads to acceptance. Acceptance leads to wisdom.

Often detachment is associated with lack of concern. However, detachment, as intended here, is the ability to create space between what you expect (which may or may not be true) and true reality.

For example, when you get called to the boss's office, you may feel anticipation, either good or bad, about the meeting. You've created an expectation. This is an ordinary human response.

Or, your birthday is coming up, and you have the hope, anticipation, expectation that your loved ones will celebrate you in some way. You've conjured up ideas of what might happen—what you want to happen, but may not have control over.

Think of a time when you've created a story, good or bad, about something you expected to happen that didn't turn out the way you anticipated. What feelings arose during that time of expectation? What feelings emerged after it didn't go the way you hoped it would?

Is it possible that you would feel more at peace if you hadn't created the story or expectation?

Self-Reflection:

How often do I move through my day with expectations of myself or others? If those expectations aren't met, how do I respond? Do I respond with judgment or acceptance?

Informal Practice:

Today I will intentionally look for instances where I have expectations. As I notice them, I will detach emotion from the outcome. I will simply accept the results and notice how this feels in my body.

Day 17: The Circular Nature of Compassion

Compassion for yourself leads to greater compassion for others. Compassion for others leads to better acceptance of yourself.

So far you've explored getting comfortable in your own skin, quieting your mind, leaning into self-acceptance, and recognizing that you are just fine exactly as you are.

Now, let's review the definition of compassion from the prologue.

Compassion combines:

1) **Awareness**—recognition of suffering or distress in self or others;

2) **Empathy**—being emotionally touched by the suffering or distress;

3) **Action**—feeling compelled to take action to help ease the suffering or distress.

Taking action can involve doing anything along a continuum, from helping at the food bank, to donating to your favorite cause, to imagining the person experiencing distress and authentically and sincerely sending well-wishes to that person.

After 16 days of exploring and acting upon the ideas shared in the book, do you see how cultivating self-acceptance and self-compassion has benefited not only you, but others in your life? Throughout this book we will expand those concepts even further via intentional compassionate acts.

Self-Reflection:

What relationship can I enhance by connecting first with compassion for myself then extending it outward? Does this idea feel exciting or uncomfortable?

Informal Practice:

Today I will practice being comfortable in my own skin. If I feel resistance to this I will extend compassion to myself. Once I have basked in compassion for myself, I will extend compassion out toward others.

Day 18: Viewing the World from Your Heart

Learn from the heart.
Don't always see from the eyes alone.

It is easy to become lulled by the busyness of life. You get wrapped up in thinking about everything you need to accomplish, keeping your brain constantly engaged.

In those moments, you forget to slow down. You fail to remember to open your heart. You lose sight of viewing the world, making decisions, or learning from a kinder, more compassionate place.

Can you remember a time when you responded to something purely from a practical, rational point of view; then after the fact realized a response from the kindness of your heart may have brought a better result?

Create a habit of considering what drives your actions. Examine why you are making certain decisions. If possible, make the choice to be moved by your heart as well as by your mind.

Contemporary research supports the benefits of viewing the world with awe and wonder. Some of the recognized benefits of seeing with our hearts, being in a state of awe, include: enhanced creativity, nurtured hope and gratitude, fostered kindness, and connection with nature.

Self-Reflection:

How would events of the past week be different if I had focused on learning and listening from my heart rather than my mind?

Informal Practice:

Today as I interact with people I will listen from my heart as well as my mind and respond from my heart when possible.

Day 19: Respect

Respect for yourself leads to respect for others. The more you respect yourself the more you will find peace.

Respect for yourself begins with acceptance of yourself. When you embrace who you are and leave behind the others' opinions, you no longer need admiration or accolades from others. As you stand self assured yet humble in your own self-acceptance you begin gaining respect from others.

Have you ever felt someone has taken advantage of you because you didn't stand up for yourself? That was an opportunity to practice self-respect. Have you ever given to others so much that you ended up becoming burned-out, resentful, or ill? That was an opportunity to practice self-respect.

You don't need to be filled with ego, or puffed up with pride to reflect self-respect. Simple, quiet acts with true intention show you have self-respect. The more often you engage with others from this quiet place of strength, the more your heart is at peace.

Self-Reflection:

Have I ever expressed disrespect for someone else, because I was uncomfortable in my own skin? Have I ever over-extended myself? How would things be different if I approached the same situation while at peace with myself?

Informal Practice:

Today, wherever I go, and whomever I encounter, I will give the gift of respect. I will accept people for who they are, and I will curtail judgment. I will prevent myself from over-extending. By doing so, I enact acceptance, kindness, respect, and peace in my life.

Day 20: Letting Go of Hardness
Being hard on yourself is easy.
Try not to do that.

Read that again. "Being hard on yourself is easy. Try not to do that." It sounds simple, doesn't it?

In reality it is simple. It is a choice. Sometimes we forget that we actually do have choices about what rattles around in our brain.

I talked with a friend recently about stress management, and he said he's much better at managing it now than he was a few months ago. I asked him what changed. He replied, "When I catch myself getting down on myself about the way something went at work, I say to myself, 'Stop thinking about that. Thinking about the problem right now in that way is not helpful. You're not taking action, and you're making up worst-case scenarios. Stop.'"

He made a choice. He was aware of what his mind was doing and he opted to redirect it.

I'm not suggesting that we suppress or deny the agitation that creates rumination. Rather, I suggest that when we notice distress we embrace it with kindness and compassion. We need to look for the underlying cause, the unmet need, of the story.

Staying connected with breath and body, and letting the mental story go, while exploring the feelings that arise while settling the mind, is a wonderful technique for learning how to be easier on ourselves.

Self-Reflection:

What would happen if I lived life from a place where what I think of me takes precedence over what others think of me?

Informal Practice:

Today I will be kind to myself while still being as productive as my day needs me to be.

Day 21: See from the Heart

Close your eyes and see from the heart.
If your heart is closed you cannot see.

Can you think of a time when you made a difficult choice and followed suggestions from your mind, when in reality a better choice may have been made by following suggestions from your heart?

We have all been there.

You can't always make heart-based decisions. It is important to be practical.

However, it is often helpful to remember to use both the heart and the mind when making decisions.

Self-Reflection:

What prevents me from being open-hearted at times?

Informal Practice:

Today I will look for random acts of kindness in the world around me.

Day 22: Forgiveness and Contentment

Contentment arises from open-hearted forgiveness.

Imagine what it might feel like if you held no resentment toward yourself or others. Imagine how freedom from bitterness might reduce stress, depression, or anxiety. Imagine the sense of contentment that would naturally arise from releasing resentment.

Often a lack of forgiveness is what holds us back from stepping into a peaceful life. We hold ourselves accountable for some past error. We hold others accountable for something said ages ago. What's the benefit? Holding grudges does not serve us.

You cannot change the past so do your best not to spend your present moments reliving it.

It takes courage to look at grudges you hold against yourself and others. It takes willingness and resilience to hold your past wrongs up to the light and to extend forgiveness.

But, once you do, it feels as if an entire burden has been lifted. You feel lighter, more at peace, and more content.

Self-Reflection:

Am I holding on to resentment toward myself or anyone else? What prevents me from offering forgiveness to myself or others? How might it feel in my body to release these resentments and open-heartedly forgive myself or others?

Informal Practice:

Today, I will find 10 minutes to sit in comfortable silence and bring to mind people for whom I feel resentment. I will connect with my heart and breathe deeply. Then I will consider one person at a time, and authentically offer forgiveness. At the end of the 10 minutes I will mentally send well-wishes to all the people I have forgiven.

Day 23: Self and Others

*How you affect yourself
is more important than how you affect others.
Be good to yourself.*

I often hear it is easier to extend kindness and compassion to others than it is to be kind and compassionate to self. This perspective is part of our current social norm.

But what would happen if you chose not to follow social norms? What if today you made a commitment to be just as kind, if not kinder, to yourself than you are to others? What would happen if you carried that perspective with you tomorrow, and the day after, and so on?

Recall for a moment some of the recent atrocities that have taken place globally.

What might have been the outcome if the people doing harm actually were kind to themselves rather than potentially angry with themselves? What might have happened if they'd accepted themselves and were willing to grow? I think events would have turned out differently, or perhaps never would have occurred at all.

Change in the world starts with each of us individually. Start with yourself. Today.

Self-Reflection:

How many days a week am I genuinely as kind to myself as I am to others?

Informal Practice:

I will treat myself as kindly today as I treat others. This may even involve asking others to help me.

Day 24: Tenderness

Don't beat yourself up.
Be tender when dealing with yourself.
It leads to being tender towards others.

When I was a kid I was hard on myself. Really hard. I don't exactly know why I decided this was good idea. Not surprisingly, it didn't feel very good. I wondered why I didn't seem to have many friends.

Then, through cultivating a compassion meditation practice, I began to realize I didn't have to treat myself that way. I didn't have to beat myself up mentally and emotionally. I began to be tender with myself.

As I did, I began to feel better. Better in my heart. Better in my mind. Better in my body.

I started to have better relationships with friends, and I let my guard down. People began to see the softer, goofier side of me. Eventually, as I became more tender with myself, that tenderness naturally began to flow outward.

Does this example sound at all familiar to you? You have the ability to create positive change for yourself. And through that change, that increased tenderness will affect your relationship with others.

Self-Reflection:

How would I feel if I genuinely accepted myself exactly as I am? Is this idea uncomfortable? Does it offer me hope? Or do I feel both?

Informal Practice:

Today, as I move through my day, I will pause now and then to gauge my level of tenderness toward myself. If I am feeling distressed or agitated I will drop my gaze, take a few deep breaths, and give myself an internal hug.

Day 25: Improving from Weakness

Recognize your weakness.
From there you can improve.

Have you ever run across people who tell grandiose stories? Stories that are almost too good to be true about all the cool places they've been, or all the money they've made, or how nothing is ever wrong with their lives?

Have you ever thought that those stories might just be cover for something else? Often that is exactly what they are. A mask for an aspect of life he or she doesn't want to examine.

One of the challenges—and joys—of cultivating a compassion meditation practice, is the willingness to look into your own heart and see everything. Not just the joy, peace, and happiness, but also the fear, anger, and resentment.

Embrace all aspects of yourself in order to truly grow. Recognize your weaknesses as well as your strengths. Once you've viewed your weaknesses with kindness and compassion, you can choose to embrace them. You can work with them, lean into them, and grow through them.

Self-Reflection:
What are my strengths? What are my weaknesses?

Informal Practice:
Today I will notice if or when I am being hard on myself. I will take a moment to breathe deeply and notice objects directly in front of me, which helps me to redirect my thoughts. I will remind myself that I am enough just as I am. I will remind myself to be kinder to myself, and to accept myself as I am.

Day 26: Stillness

*From stillness comes the ability
to see from the heart.
Heaven is in the heart; feel it.*

Have you ever come across a completely still pool of water? One so still the line between what is beneath the surface and what reflects off the surface becomes blurred? It is an amazing thing to see. I always feel awe when I see water like that.

When you allow your own mind to become still, something similar happens.

You see the beauty in yourself. You appreciate the stillness of your mind and the depth of your breath. In these still moments, you deeply connect with your heart. As you do, the light from within your heart begins to shine outward.

As your heart shines outward all the beauty of the world is reflected back to you, illuminated by the glow of your kindness, acceptance, and stillness.

Self-Reflection:

How would my life be different if I spent 10 minutes or more a day without distraction (no computers, devices, phones, books)? How would it feel in my body if my mind was still?

Informal Practice:

Today I will take 10 minutes or more and be free from devices and distractions. I will go for a walk, or sit on the deck listening to birds, or relax watching the rustling leaves. I will allow myself to be still, and revel in the beauty that fills my heart.

Day 27: Humility

*Humility is having knowledge
but no desire to show it.
Strive to be humble.*

I love it when I talk with people and I feel like they're authentically being themselves, speaking their truth simply and without bragging.

You have something valuable to say. Sometimes you might not feel that way, and end up covering things over with exaggeration to impress others. But that exaggeration is just a mask.

When you lean into acceptance, you know you are enough. You don't need to compete. You aren't worried about other people's opinions. As you move more fully into this place of self-acceptance, you can truly be humble.

When you accept yourself and have knowledge about something, you share it with grace. You don't need to show off. You simply speak from the heart with humility, and let the truth found in that action speak louder than words.

Self-Reflection:

Do I ever exaggerate when I don't need to? What benefit do I gain from this behavior? What might be the downside?

Informal Practice:

Today I will be genuine and humble in my inter-actions with others.

Day 28: Comparing to Others

Don't compare yourself to others.
Know you are enough.

Have you heard of imposter syndrome, a term coined in 1978 by clinical psychologists Dr. Pauline R. Clance and Suzanne A. Imes? It's when you feel like you're a fraud in the face of peers because you haven't internalized your successes.

An astonishingly large number of people in the United States (and I'd bet worldwide) experience impostor syndrome at one time or another.

I was working with a group in a high-performance corporate setting and the question was asked, "How many of you have experienced imposter syndrome at least once in your life?" Every hand in the room went up. Wow! From my perspective, these were some of the best and brightest minds out there—and they felt like frauds.

Those raised hands highlight the tremendous value of being comfortable in our own skins. Internally acknowledge and appreciate your accomplishments—without comparison to others.

It doesn't matter what the person next to you has done. What matters is what you have done. No matter how big or small. You have done it. Be proud of yourself.

It takes practice to reframe your thinking. It takes diligence to develop a new mindset. It takes resilience to develop self-acceptance.

It is your choice. Embrace yourself for all you have done and all you will do.

Self-Reflection:

How do I describe the difference between self-acceptance and self-esteem?

Informal Practice:

Today I will celebrate my successes without concern for what anyone else thinks of me or those successes.

Day 29: Embrace this Moment

Acceptance is, "I can do more, but in the meantime I will embrace this moment."

Embracing this moment is not an easy thing to do, and it doesn't happen overnight. But as you sit with yourself and settle your mind, you begin looking at all the elements floating beneath the surface of your emotions and thoughts. No matter what you see, you can choose to lean into it. Remember the deep, dark water that had turtles rather than sharks?

Embrace all the wonderful, joyful "stuff" of yourself. Contemplate all the challenging and icky parts as well. With practice and patience your neural networks become rewired, and self-acceptance becomes the norm not the exception.

As you move into self-acceptance and embrace your humanity, you recognize that others have challenges as well. Just like you, they have wonderful bits and icky bits. As you soften judgment for yourself, you soften judgment for others. This leads to open-hearted acceptance.

Self-Reflection:

How often am I content in this moment without thinking I need to be doing more?

Informal Practice:

Today if I notice I am feeling stressed out about deadlines, I will return my thoughts to the present moment and continue with what I am doing.

Day 30: Accepting Challenge

Acceptance of self leads to acceptance of others and challenging situations.

As you deepen your meditation practice and become more comfortable in your own skin, you also cultivate self-acceptance. As you become willing to accept yourself in all circumstances, you expand your ability to accept others.

Not only does this relaxed, accepting state of mind apply to personalities and people, it applies to challenging situations as well.

Years ago a little 2-wheel-drive car my friends and I rented got stuck on a sand road in Namibia in Skeleton Coast National Park. We could have worried, and maybe we did a little. But we weren't incredibly worried. We figured somehow things would work out.

But we never anticipated that two rotund National Park employees, dressed in pale green coveralls, would drive up in their truck. They hopped out, ran over to the front of our car, backs to the hood, lifted the whole front end out of the sand, and rotated the car 90 degrees. Without a word they jogged back to their truck and drove off.

I love this story as an illustration for how acceptance of, rather than resistance to, challenging situations may lead to unexpected and positive results.

Self-Reflection:

What is my typical reaction when I find myself in a challenging situation? How can I change that, if necessary, to be more accepting of self and/or others?

Informal Practice:

Today I will embrace challenging situations with an open heart rather than a closed mind.

Day 31: Know You Are Enough

Know you are enough.
From there, rise above all challenges.

The first step to creating a positive mindset or happier outlook—whatever you prefer to call it—is acknowledging that you have choice about what is going on in your head.

You can choose whether or not to mentally re-hash that fight with your friend last week, or be anxious about your upcoming review. You can choose whether or not to be pissed off at the current state of politics in the USA or the world.

Knowing that you can turn off the autopilot—that you have a choice about what occupies your head—is the first step to discovering peace of mind.

When you have peace of mind, when you are comfortable in your own skin, you can discontinue proving points, refuting others, and defensive behavior. You have the resilience to harmonize with what surrounds you.

Self-Reflection:

What does my body feel like when I am not kind to myself?

Informal Practice:

Today, I will look in the mirror and tell myself that I am enough just the way I am, and that I will continue to grow and become even better.

Day 32: Active Minds

An active mind creates demons out of nothing.

Choosing to control what occupies your mind takes patience, courage, and practice. Often it is easier to let your mind run wild rather than reining it in.

An acquaintance recently told me, sometimes in quiet moments, her mind replays stories of past wrongs. As she replays these stories, she begins to feel worse about not only other people but herself as well. Then her mind shifts from relationships gone awry to how horrible she must be as a human being.

I don't know her well, but from the little I do know I think she is a vibrant, intelligent, successful woman. Clearly when her mind goes wild, that isn't the way she perceives herself.

I recommended she try using the 4-part-breath technique for a few days when she noticed negative stories (see Day 2). I suggested she practice patience with herself in the process. I asked her not to give up. I encouraged her to face the difficulties, sitting with those stories and looking at what might be the underlying unmet needs—in herself or others.

When we talked again the next week she said she felt much better. She felt lighter, happier, and more at ease. And, she found she didn't fear having quiet moments the way she did before.

You do have choice over what fills your mind. What you practice becomes the norm. You can train yourself to be kinder, gentler, and more at peace.

Self-Reflection:

How often do I let my mind run wild? When it does, does it drift toward the negative? What would it feel like in my body if I were to harness my mind and gently and kindly stop those negative stories?

Informal Practice:

Today I will observe the choices I make in each moment. Noticing these choices brings me into present moment awareness. Present moment awareness helps prevent ruminating about the past or worrying about the future.

Day 33: Duality

To thrive you must be aware of your negative side, but function from the positive side. Accept the good, but do not reject the bad.

A new friend recently told me she feels out of touch with her emotions. She was brought up in an environment that encouraged her to always project a pleasant or happy persona. She knew sometimes she was angry, or sad, or fearful, but perpetually put those emotions aside and projected a positive mask.

As a result she felt pretty stressed out and emotionally numb.

It takes effort and courage to look at those less-positive emotions. It is easy to suppress or deny behavior you do not value.

However, to grow and thrive, you must move beyond projecting solely a positive outlook. Observe all of your behaviors, emotions, and moods. When you see something you don't care for, explore the potential cause.

Take a look deep into your heart and see the fear, anger, and resentment. Then, with courage, embrace these emotions. Look at them. Sit down and share a cup of tea with them. Recognize what those emotions feel like in your body.

Duality is everywhere in nature. To thrive, you need to look at and embrace all aspects of yourself.

Self-Reflection:

When you are being self-critical/self-judgmental what are the consequences of being hard on yourself? How does it feel in your body? Do you find it motivates you or makes you discouraged?

Informal Practice:

Today when I make a choice, I will ask myself two questions:

1) What are the consequences of this choice I am making?

2) Will this choice bring fulfilment and happiness to me as well as those around me?

Day 34: Try Until You Succeed

When attempting to create change,
if you don't succeed, do not stop trying.
Continue trying until you do succeed.

Have you ever noticed days when you your wheels are spinning and you're not getting anywhere? Days when you feel a little constricted or closed up? Perhaps you feel a little stiff, inflexible, and certainly not fluid, joyful, ready to see the beauty in anything.

When I notice that feeling, physically and emotionally, I kindly remind myself that everything will end up being fine. I feel better when I'm not stressed out about getting the project done. I soften both my attitude and my body.

I look for something that makes me smile—the birdsong out my window, a happy dog on a walk with his guardian, the leaves fluttering in the breeze. I breathe into and out from my heart. I stretch a little, and I consciously relax my shoulders and neck.

Then slowly, bit by bit, I feel better both in body and mind. I find my wheels don't spin as much. I'm able to get traction. And, I'm pleased because I didn't give up.

How do you feel in your body, heart, and mind when you're trying to create change and get stuck?

Self-Reflection:
Do I tend to finish projects I start? If not, why not?

Informal Practice:
Today, if I come across something challenging, something I might typically set aside or give up on, I will stick with it until I have moved through the challenge or come to resolution.

Day 35: Seeing in the Dark

*Seeing in the dark comes from the light
of our heart. The light of our heart
comes only through acceptance of self.*

As you cultivate your compassion meditation practice you realize that you have something very special inside of you. You have an internal dimension that is solely your own. You honor that unique inner-wisdom through faith and belief in yourself.

The practices of awareness, empathy, respect, and simple kindness create a compassionate heart. Helping others is critical to living a generous, compassionate life. You must also realize the importance of extending this generosity of spirit to yourself. Be tolerant of your mistakes, failings, and flaws. Cultivate goodwill, both inwardly and outwardly.

When you help other people, you offer yourself. If you don't like and care for yourself, how can you fully offer yourself to others?

You extend support and love to your family and friends through the traits of trustworthiness, steadfastness, reliability, and presence. Connect with your internal light and let it shine forth.

Self-Reflection:

In what circumstance did I know compassion for another was the right course of action, but I did not follow that course? What were the barriers in that instance? In what circumstance did I know compassion for myself was the right course of action, but I did not follow that course? What were the barriers in that instance?

Informal Practice:

Today I will pay attention to how my body feels throughout the day, with particular attention paid to any physical responses to emotional states.

Day 36: Vulnerability

*Vulnerability offers us the opportunity
to learn about ourselves.*

Vulnerability is often misunderstood as weakness. However, it takes courage and strength to be vulnerable. It takes willingness to admit you don't know it all or that you might need help. It takes courage not to blame others for things which happen to you.

Through exploring your vulnerability, you learn about your own internal strength. You become resilient in the face of challenge. You learn that you can let go of blame and judgment. You learn to recognize that sometimes you are stronger when connected to community than you are on your own.

When you look tenderly at the places inside you that cause discomfort, and then extend compassion and kindness to those places, you begin healing old wounds. If you don't look at those places, if you don't embrace your vulnerability, you may end up becoming hard, inflexible, and judgmental.

Take the time to embrace vulnerability. Learn how to be soft and resilient at the same time.

Self-Reflection:

What are my biggest fears around expressing vulnerability? How often do I put on a strong outer face or presence when I am actually feeling small inside?

Informal Practice:

Today I will practice letting my guard down. I will ask for help when I need it. I will admit when I don't know the answer.

Day 37: What Sticks to Us

*What we do to ourselves matters more
than what others do to us.*

At one time or another someone will say something
mean, rude, or disrespectful to you. It is part of life.
It is part of being human.

We have a choice about how to respond. We could
hang onto those mean words for years, and often we
do. Sometimes we react by lashing back, and often
we do. However, we could choose a different action.

When those instances come up, try taking a
moment to breathe. Pausing for that moment can
help you respond rather than react. It creates a bit of
a gap between someone else's unskillful action, and
your action. It is up to you to decide if you want to
react or respond.

Often, if you react—when you send that snarky
email written in haste, or say something hurtful
that you really might not mean—that reaction sticks
with you. You mull it over after the fact, wishing you
might be able to take back those words or actions.

Cultivating patience, taking a moment for a deep
breath or two, creates that opportunity to respond
well—to respond with grace. Perhaps you will even
surprise the other person with the lack of a snarky
comeback. Ultimately your action is what you live
with every day.

Focus on making your part of a situation a
response rather than a reaction.

Self-Reflection:

How much consideration do I give to what others think of me? How does that influence how I think of myself?

Informal Practice:

Three times throughout the day today I will repeat for myself: I am safe. I am at ease. I am kind to myself and accept myself as I am. I am filled with peace and joy.

CULTIVATING PEACE

Day 38: Peace with Yourself

Your responsibility
is to be at peace with yourself.

It sounds simple doesn't it? However, it certainly isn't easy.

As you deepen your compassion meditation practice and become more aware of your emotions and needs, and as you authentically believe and accept that you are enough just as you are, the idea of being at peace with yourself becomes easier.

One benefit of meditation is, with practice, you clear away the mental clutter and constant chatter in your head. As that clutter clears, you have more space, more quiet. In those quiet moments, seeds of internal peace begin growing.

Remind yourself that you have a choice about how you feel in the moment. You may not be able to change current circumstances, but with practice you have complete control over how you react to those circumstances. Continue to consciously move toward being at peace.

Sometimes clearing the physical chaos of clutter in your home reduces mental turmoil as well. Responsibly maintaining your environment may bring peace of mind.

Self-Reflection:

Do I have any physical "stuff" in my life that I could recycle, give away, or take to the dump? How would creating more "space" feel in my heart and body?

Informal Practice:

Today I will clean out a drawer, a closet, or a room, and embrace the sense of peace that comes with releasing clutter.

Day 39: Perspective and Peace

See the good in everything.
Then you will find peace.

Again, the above is simple to say, but not always easy to do.

Remember that you have choice over your outlook. As you deepen your compassion meditation practice, you change your ability to interact with your circumstances.

You may not be able to change the circumstances, but you can always choose how to respond.

Take the time to be aware of the present moment. Make the choice to enjoy whatever occurs. Remember you have the ability to find peace in your world.

No one can guarantee you a peace-filled life, but you can create one if you choose to see the good in everything.

Self-Reflection:

How often do I look for the good in daily life?

Informal Practice:

Today I will practice seeing the good in everything. As part of the process of seeing the good, I will also extend unexpected kindness to someone.

Day 40: Time Famine

If you have patience
you will find the wisdom in things.

I recently heard the phrase "**time famine**," a term developed in 1999 by professor Leslie A. Perlow, as a way to describe the sensation that comes when we have a huge "to do" list without feeling like we have enough time to get it all done.

I know that feeling. On the whole though, I'm pretty happy, as my list doesn't overwhelm me. I'm able to separate myself from it, and recognize that I'm still okay if I don't get everything done in some made-up time frame.

I've learned over the years to recognize when I feel the symptoms of "time famine." At those times I need to extend patience to myself. Through that patience, I've found the wisdom to be at peace with what I can get done hour by hour.

This idea of using patience to find the wisdom in things can be used in many instances. For example, have you ever written then sent a reactionary email in response to something that upset you? If so, afterward, when you cooled off, did you ever wish you'd not sent it?

Have you ever been frustrated by really wanting something to happen—a new job, or car, or relationship—but it didn't turn out the way you wanted? In hindsight were you ever grateful things didn't work out?

Those feelings and responses are part of being human. Remember to be patient. Allow life to unfold at its own pace.

Self-Reflection:

How patient am I? Do I usually wait for things to unfold? Or do I try to "force" things to happen?

Informal Practice:

Today, if something is not going as quickly as I would like, or others are not getting back to me as soon as I want, I will practice patience.

Day 41: Taking the Easy Way

It is easy to make things difficult.
Try to make things simple.

Years ago I received a scholarship to study abroad for a year. I narrowed my choices down to universities in Kenya, and New Zealand. In the same week I received acceptance letters from both. If I went to Kenya I'd have only 6 weeks before departure. If I went to New Zealand I'd have 6 months to prepare.

I went to breakfast with a friend and expressed my conundrum. He asked, "What do you want to do with your free time?" I said I wanted to be outside exploring nature. He responded, "I have spent time in Nairobi. You won't easily find what you're looking for there. I've also been to New Zealand. Access to what you want will be much easier."

Then he followed with the real zinger...

"Since I've known you, you usually choose the most difficult option. You don't have to beat your head against a wall all the time. You can use this opportunity to learn something new, and have fun exploring. You can make things simple."

Wow! The things we don't see in ourselves. I hadn't realized I gravitated toward the most difficult choice, but he was right. I just needed to hear it from someone else. I ended up choosing New Zealand, and had one of the best years of my life.

These days, when I have difficult choices to make, I sometimes recall that breakfast. I think about whether the simple answer will be not only less difficult but equally fulfilling.

Self-Reflection:

How often do I make things more difficult than they have to be?

Informal Practice:

Today, at least once, I will act on the simpler choice.

Day 42: Letting Go of Grumpiness

Being grumpy doesn't serve any purpose.
Find a way to entertain yourself; be light.

Do you ever find yourself reveling in being a grouch? In a weird way, occasionally it just feels good to be cranky. At times we truly do need to be cranky in order to honor our authentic feelings. Sometimes our hormones have taken over, and we don't have much control over being cranky.

However, the benefits to grumpiness have limits.

On those days when you notice you're grouchy, and you've made peace with it but are still hanging onto those grumpy feelings; check in with yourself to see if that state of being continues to serve you.

If not, remember you have a choice. You can choose to change your mindset. A technique that may be helpful is to bring vividly to mind an image of something you really enjoy. Choose an image that fills your heart with awe, peace, pleasure, or joy. It could be an image of a loved one, a scene from nature, a pet, a wise person you deeply respect, or a time in your life when you experienced something active and enjoyable.

Bringing to mind an image and focusing on it, while breathing deeply, helps break that mental cycle of grumpiness.

Self-Reflection:

When I find myself being grumpy, what action do I take to change my mood? If I do not take any action, why not?

Informal Practice:

Today, if I find a moment of grumpiness, I will bring to mind an image that makes my heart happy; and I will breathe deeply and fully for a few breaths while holding this image in mind.

Day 43: Faith in the Future

If you truly live in the present moment, you must have faith that the future will take care of itself.

Sometimes it is hard to have faith in something outside your control. However, when you let your mind relax and your heart open, you will often find that unexpected good comes your way.

Preparing for the future is valuable. Nevertheless, you also need to have faith or belief that the future will take care of itself. Without that faith, you would become mired in endless worry about things over which you have no control.

When you find yourself anxious about the future, take a moment to connect with your body and take a few deep breaths. Give yourself an internal hug. Relax your mind. Open your heart. Trust. From this place of surrender and acceptance, peace transcends.

Self-Reflection:

How often do I worry about the future? How much of that time is spent thinking about things over which I actually have no control?

Informal Practice:

Today when I notice that I'm thinking anxiously about the future, I will remind myself that it is just a story and bring myself back to the present moment. If I am creating a productive action plan for the future, I will write it down, and then return to the present moment.

Day 44: Understanding

Understanding leads to compassion.
Compassion leads to peace.

The more you look at all aspects of your heart—the comfortable places as well as the places that scare you—the more you fully understand who you are. As you begin peeling away layers you present to others, you arrive at the central truth of your beliefs.

By exploring your beliefs, and holding them up to the light, you become more straightforward, reliable, caring, and sincere. Through standing on a strong foundation of your principles, you deepen your relationships with yourself and your family. You develop genuine friendships with others.

Work toward understanding your own beliefs. Then act upon them, even in challenging times. As you do, you become more accepting of yourself and others. As your acceptance grows, you become filled with peace.

Self-Reflection:

How often do I fully listen to others without forming a response or question in my head before they have completed what they are saying?

Informal Practice:

Today I will practice being present with people and truly listen to what they say. I will listen with acceptance rather than judgment.

Day 45: Embrace New Experiences

Don't hang on to experiences.
Each new experience brings life.

As you cultivate your compassion meditation practice, you become more accepting of yourself and your life. You begin learning how to detach.

This does not mean that you don't care about things, people, or your responsibilities. You still experience strong emotions and can be deeply involved with other people. But you learn to maintain perspective, to see things in context rather than merely from the narrow viewpoint of your ego.

When someone infuriates you, you still feel the rage. In addition, however, you cultivate the discipline to view the situation impersonally, as if you were an impartial observer. You learn to feel your emotions, but not be attached to them. You may experience deep grief at the death of a loved one, but you don't define yourself by that emotion. You can be in mourning, yet still experience joy.

Learn to detach from your past patterns of behavior. Some people define themselves as victims for whom everything seems to go wrong, as scapegoats who are always picked on, as under-achievers, or as overachievers. Try not to define or limit yourself in terms of stereotypes or anything else. Learn to detach yourself from your own destructive habits.

This detachment allows you to open your heart and cultivates willingness to learn and grow from new experiences.

Self-Reflection:

How often do I replay past favorite moments while forgetting the beauty of this present moment?

Informal Practice:

Today I will try or do something new that I haven't done before. It could be eating a new food, brushing my teeth with my non-dominant hand, taking a walk in a new park. I open-heartedly look forward to creating a new experience.

Day 46: Peace
Find peace with whatever you do.

Spinning negative stories in your head, leads to discontent. Everyone does it.

Recognizing stories as they're happening requires you to be present. Present moment awareness and meditation help you break this cycle.

When minds spin, they often create stories about the past or future. The past is in the past, so unless you're creating an action to plan to resolve what has already taken place, there is little point in ruminating about it.

The future is in the future. While constructive planning is beneficial, if you're creating disaster stories, remember that they are just stories.

I know a couple of people who are disaster-preppers. Though it is valuable to have supplies on hand for an emergency, there is a downside to spending emotional and mental energy worrying non-stop about the next earthquake or flood.

When you notice you're telling yourself stories in your head, check in with yourself to see if they're making you feel peaceful or anxious. If these stories are not serving you well, acknowledge them (rather than suppressing or denying them) and put them to rest.

Self-Reflection:

What does having peace of mind mean to me?

Informal Practice:

Today I will practice patience with myself and others. I will notice the sense of peace that comes with patience.

Day 47: Rise Above Smallness

Suffering is universal.
Rising above suffering is essential.
Rise above your own smallness of life.

We all do it at one time or another—we throw ourselves a pity party. We all revel in our pain, grief, anger, fear. Sometimes it simply feels good to roll around in the muck of our minds—for a moment.

But don't stay there indefinitely. If you roll around in the muck too long, it begins to act like quicksand and holds on tight. It begins to suck you down, slowly, bit by bit.

In those moments it is critical to move toward solid ground. You must reach for the rope that is thrown to you, or have the strength of will to push yourself up and out of the pit on your own.

You have only one life to live. Live it joyfully, passionately, and with purpose. You must look at, recognize, and embrace your challenges. Learn from them, grow from them, and become resilient.

That is why you cultivate acceptance and compassion for self and others. You cultivate these perspectives to gain awareness of your own suffering. Awareness allows you to explore and work through your difficulties, helping you attain peace of mind. From this quiet peace you begin helping others.

Self-Reflection:

When feel stressed out, blue, or in pain, how often do I remember that I am not alone in my distress?

Informal Practice:

Today, if difficulty arises, I will remind myself that others have experienced similar challenges. If I notice someone else is experiencing difficulty, I will offer help in whatever way that person needs, knowing I may have been challenged the same way in the past.

Day 48: Simplicity Is Good

Do simple things
and life will not be so difficult.

Cultivating a meditation practice doesn't always have to be hard work. Growing as an individual doesn't always have to be a struggle.

Tremendous value and benefit can be found in doing simple things. One way to help your mind, body, and heart feel better, is to go outside.

Get some fresh air. Get a bit of sunshine, or breeze, or gentle rain on your face. Connect with something that is growing. Take a walk.

Whether you live near a park, a forest, the water, or in the city, look for something that is green and alive. Listen to the birds. Notice the temperature and the humidity.

Embrace the simplicity of this idea.

Self-Reflection:

What is my favorite way to connect with nature? How can I connect with nature on a daily basis? How does my body feel when I do?

Informal Practice:

At the end of the day I will recall the simplest thing I did today and appreciate the ease of that task/conversation.

Day 49: Doing

Focus on what you "do,"
rather than on what you "need to do."
"Need to do" is an endless list.

Our lives are filled with "to do" lists. We regularly think of or plan for the future. Future planning is important, but we also need to remember the value of focusing on this moment.

A friend once told me that he realized his "to do" list was endless. It was so long he ultimately gave up on doing anything because he was overwhelmed. He felt progress eluded him.

Then he realized that by taking 3 things on his list and creating a separate, small list, he could actually complete his list. So each day he would select 3 things. He'd write them down. He'd give himself the freedom to take as much time as each needed. When each was completed he'd cross it off the list.

He began to feel better. He suddenly felt like he was both more productive and had more free time. His confidence in his actions grew, and he felt more at peace. When he finished the three things, he might do more. Or, he might not. He was at peace with either choice, because he'd finished what he'd set out to do.

Finally he realized he was feeling better because he was getting things done, and at the same time he also focused on the present moment. He paid attention to the "do" and not the "need to do." He recognized the value of simplifying complex tasks, and being content in the present moment.

Self-Reflection:

How often does my mind drift to the future rather than staying in the present? What is the benefit of staying in this moment?

Informal Practice:

Today I will make a "to do" list of only 3 things. I will be content when I finish them, and overjoyed if I get more done.

Day 50: Joy

See wisdom in the joy of living.

Sometimes when I'm in a coffee shop, or in line at the grocery store, or anywhere where people might be interacting, I eavesdrop. Just a little. Just to get a snippet of what is on people's minds. Sometimes I even observe topics of conversation that come up among my friends.

You know what I often hear? Fear. It might show up as something else at the surface level of the conversation, but the underlying current is fear.

You know what I don't hear? Joy. Most of the time people don't discuss the incredible beauty they've just witnessed. Mostly people aren't talking about how excited and happy they are to be living the lives they're leading.

It is your responsibility to start spreading the word about joy. It is your way to contribute to society's positive growth.

When you embody and express joy you feel better within yourself. By expressing joy you also contribute to the creation of healthier communities.

Look for the joy around you. Express the joy that is within you. Share it with others.

Self-Reflection:

When was the last time I took five minutes to stand in awe of nature? How did that feel in my body?

Informal Practice:

Today I will strive to feel joyful. I will cultivate joy within me, and I will express it outwardly by smiling at others, and engaging in positive, uplifting conversations. I will help others remember to connect with joy.

Day 51: Harmony

*Every day find internal harmony
and avoid conflict with yourself.*

Looking for ways to find harmony within? Start by taking a few deep breaths in through the nose all the way down into your belly, allowing the belly to relax as you inhale. Then follow the movement in the body as you bring the breath back up from the belly through the chest and out the mouth. Simply tune into the feelings in the body.

Allow your body to relax deeply, letting your muscles soften. Allow your mind to settle and your heart to open. Harmonize your body and mind.

Connect with something outside of yourself. Engage with nature. Listen for the birdsong, or the sound of a breeze in the trees outside your window. Look for a spot of green, either outside or inside, if you have potted plants.

Take responsibility for yourself in this moment. You are in charge. Your mind is still, and your heart is open. Know that every problem is an opportunity in disguise.

This is how to be at peace, in harmony, and minimize internal conflict.

Self-Reflection:

If I am at peace with myself, how might I better help others?

Informal Practice:

Today, if I notice I am telling myself negative stories, I will drop my gaze and take a few deep breaths. If I notice that my inner critic pipes up, I will acknowledge it and listen to it; then I will invite it to sit quietly beside me.

Day 52: Start Your Day Right
Start every day with something good in it.

Do you start your day jarred awake with an alarm, then immediately check your phone for messages? Do you shuffle off to the shower like a robot and eat breakfast without even tasting it? Many people do.

Morning often sets the tone for the rest of the day. Enjoying your morning is important, even when you feel like you're swamped with other tasks.

Regardless of how you choose to do it, make a point of starting every day with something good in it. Notice how the rest of your day goes from there.

Self-Reflection:

How often do I wake up in a good mood? How long does that mood last?

Informal Practice:

Today I will offer myself a genuine heartfelt smile in the mirror. I will say to myself via my reflection, "I am a good person, and I am happy about that."

Day 53: A Rich Life
A simple life is a rich life.

One day some friends and I visited a rural home just outside of Lhasa, Tibet. The home was constructed of mud brick with a few timbers for structure. The house had only a handful of rooms surrounding a central courtyard.

The walls were brightly painted. Flowers hung in pots. In the middle of the courtyard was a kettle perched on a simple stand surrounded by a reflective metal shield.

The owners of the home knew we were visiting and wanted to offer us tea. The sun heated the tea-water on their solar cooker.

Our hosts had radiant smiles as they handed us tea in cracked cups. It was clear they enjoyed their life and were pleased to share the afternoon, their home, and their tea with us.

At the end of the afternoon, I left their home with fond memories and a deep appreciation for the simplicity and richness of their life.

Self-Reflection:

How much "stuff" (in terms of material goods) do I need to be happy?

Informal Practice:

Today I will look for and appreciate the beauty of simplicity around me—the shape of a cloud, the color of a flower, the sun on my face, or the smell of the rain.

Day 54: End Your Day in Peace

Make peace with yourself
every night before bed.

No matter what has happened during your day today, tomorrow is a fresh new start. If for some reason today wasn't a great day for you, make peace with yourself before going to sleep. If it was a spectacular day, again, make peace with yourself before going to sleep.

Cultivate your ability to be comfortable in your own skin. Know that you are good enough today but will aspire to be even better tomorrow. It is important to express gratitude throughout the day. This is a wonderful technique to help you to be at peace before you go to sleep.

As you settle into bed, take a moment to review your day. Find contentment in the highlights, and take a moment to embrace the lowlights.

If you had a challenging day, free yourself from the need to construct stories about how things might have gone differently or better. Simply acknowledge the challenges, and remind yourself that you are human. Just like you, people all around the world have had a challenging day. And, just like you, they're all human. Remember that tomorrow is a fresh start.

Take a few deep breaths, relax your body, and express gratitude—gratitude for being alive, gratitude for having a place to lay your head, and gratitude that you have a whole new day tomorrow to learn, grow, and explore.

Self-Reflection:

How often do I go to bed anxious or upset? If it is often, what do I need to do to make peace with myself every night?

Informal Practice:

Before going to sleep I will list three or more things from today for which I am grateful.

EXTENDING COMPASSION TO OTHERS

Day 55: Function from Kindness

Function from kindness.
It is not always easy to do, but do your best.

Are you ever ill-tempered with someone (or even yourself) when there is no reason for it? This is one of those moods that may creep up on you when you're not paying attention.

One solution is to be more mindfully aware of the moment. Catch yourself before you say something or act in a certain way and ask yourself, "Am I being kind by saying or doing this? Does it contribute to the situation? Is it beneficial? Is it most kind?" If the answer to any of those questions is no, then reconsider your action.

Another solution, when you're on the verge of being unkind, is to take a moment to check in with the underlying unmet need. Is something else going on that drives your desire to act in an unkind way? For example have you ever been mad about something at work, and that translates to yelling at your dog? Have you been frustrated with your friend, so you snap at your spouse?

Whenever you're being short-tempered, take a moment to breathe and consider the true cause of the distress. After that pause, determine the best course of action, responding rather than reacting.

It isn't easy to be kind at all times, but aspire to be as kind as possible. Move through your days with kindness as your intention. With practice you will find it becomes second nature. Expressing kindness regularly leads to greater peace and contentment.

Self-Reflection:

What is the kindest thing I can do for myself today?
What kindness can I extend to someone else?

Informal Practice:

Today, if I find myself being unkind to myself or others, I will take a moment to see if I can figure out the unmet need underlying my behavior.

Day 56: Curtailing Criticism

Don't make fun of anyone.
Curtail your criticism and judgment of others.

Do you know people who constantly complain and rarely say anything good about others? Do you act like that yourself sometimes? We all do. Unfortunately, it is a pretty common response to the world. But, we can choose not to behave that way.

As you cultivate appreciation and acceptance of yourself, your capacity to appreciate others for who they are expands.

Consider that unskillful behavior may arise from unmet needs. Before you criticize someone else, take a moment to think of what really might be driving the behavior that you find challenging.

Is that person lonely, bored, angry, hungry, or anxious? If you consider the humanity in the other person, perhaps you'll find that extending some warmth, rather than criticism, helps you become more peaceful. This may not work in all circumstances, but it is worth trying. If you still choose to judge and criticize, take a closer look at what unmet need is behind your choices.

Undoubtedly some people's actions may seem unforgivable, but, in day-to-day circumstances, see if you can take a moment to recognize that we're all human, and as such, we have similar basic needs. This may help you curtail your criticism and judgment of others. As you do, see if you find a greater sense of peace within yourself.

Self-Reflection:

Am I often critical of myself or others? How does this feel in my body? How do I break this cycle?

Informal Practice:

Today I will practice non-judgment. I will notice when I am being critical of myself or others, and I will stop that cycle by taking a few deep breaths, bringing awareness to my body, and then shifting into a mindset of acceptance.

Day 57: Nobody's Perfect

Accept your own imperfection.
Accept imperfection in others. Don't have the
expectation that others should be perfect.

Patience. Tolerance. Understanding. Acceptance. How often do you think of, or act on, these words each day? Do you start with yourself? Do you aspire toward self-acceptance?

Does that inner critic continue to nag you? If so, try to become aware of when that voice arises. Listen to it to see why it is really talking to you. Give it a hug and ask it to sit quietly next to you as you move on throughout your day.

Be willing to accept that you're human, and as such, you are not perfect all the time. At the same time strive to do your best. Continue to grow. Be willing to accept imperfections as they arise.

As you extend acceptance to yourself, you become more tolerant and patient with your own imperfections. You then become more patient, tolerant, and understanding of others. This, in turn, leads to greater self-acceptance.

Taking action in this way becomes an ever-expanding spiral.

Self-Reflection:

When was the last time I gossiped about someone? How do I feel about it now? What was the benefit of gossiping about someone? What was the downside?

Informal Practice:

Today, if I or others do not "perform to my standards," I will simply appreciate what I or they did do, and extend well-wishes.

Day 58: Extending Your Heart

*The essence of beauty is the extension
of the heart. Anything done from the heart
will have impact.*

Throughout the past days we've discussed developing present moment awareness. This awareness
allows you to be more comfortable in your own skin,
which in turn leads to enhanced acceptance of
yourself and others. These subtle (or maybe not so
subtle) changes cultivate open-heartedness.

When you're open in both body and heart to what
presents itself in your day, you see more beauty in
your surroundings. When you extend your best-self
to the world, without expectation of anything in
return, you create beauty.

Have you ever had a stranger smile at you or say
a warm hello? Did that simple action brighten that
moment, or even your whole day? That was an
extension of beauty. Have you ever extended a smile
or hello to a stranger on the street? That too was an
extension of beauty.

You never know how much value a kind word, or
a smile, or opening a door might bring to someone
else. It doesn't really matter that you know. What
matters is that you're living life with an open-heart.
You're extending your inner beauty. It does have an
impact.

Self-Reflection:

When was the last time I genuinely thanked someone for doing something kind for me, even when that action was part of doing his/her job?

Informal Practice:

Each time I meet or pass someone today I will connect with my heart and offer a silent wish for happiness, joy, and health to that person.

Day 59: Listening with Your Heart

When listening to someone, connect with your heart. Then speak from your heart. This leads to greater respect.

Have you ever talked with someone, and felt like the other person wasn't listening? Frustrating, isn't it?

Have you ever felt a sense of disconnection, or perhaps lack of respect, from the other person?

Can you remember a time when someone was sharing with you, but you really didn't have the capacity or interest to listen in that moment? Think about how your inattentive listening affected the other person. Does it come across as disinterested or disrespectful? Maybe. Likely.

Given that you can control only your side of the conversation, how do you become a better listener? Being present, fully aware of the other person, is a great place to start. When you are present, you are less distracted with the stories in your own head. Then, truly listen—listen with your heart.

If advice is not asked for, don't formulate a response while the other person is speaking. If comparison isn't warranted, don't come up with stories of how "that same thing" happened to you.

Simply listen—with all of your attention, and all of your heart. When you've listened with your heart, you can then offer an authentic, heart-felt response.

Lastly, if you're not able to be present with the other person, do him or her the courtesy of saying that you are unable to listen just now. Sharing that bit of information also is a way of extending respect.

Self-Reflection:

How do I listen to another person's perspective without giving up my own? If we disagree, do I become defensive, or remain open-hearted?

Informal Practice:

Today I will truly listen to others. I will give full attention, listen from my heart, and allow others space to say what they want to say. I will be patient. If I am not able to do this, I will politely let them know I do not have time to listen right now and ask to have the conversation later.

Day 60: Harmonious Solutions

For every problem there is a solution.
Make the solution harmonious.

When you're feeling troubled, do you sometimes feel like you're the only one experiencing that particular problem? Do you sometimes feel isolated?

Connecting with someone else may be the key to finding the solution to your current troubles, even if that connection doesn't seem directly related. Through extending kindness to someone else, you may get out of your own stuck-mind.

The act of making someone else happy, extending even the smallest of kindnesses to another, helps you feel better about yourself and gives you a refreshed perspective.

Hold a door for someone. Smile and say hello to someone. Give your dog an extra snuggle.

All of these actions help you move beyond yourself, creating a sense of connection with the world around you.

Self-Reflection:

How often do I spend time looking at the negative aspect of things rather than seeing the positive? What would be the benefit of changing to a positive outlook?

Informal Practice:

Today I will focus on solutions rather than problems. I will look for ways to connect with others regardless of whether or not they help provide solutions to current challenges.

Day 61: Take Care of Yourself

Caring itself is love. Caring starts with self,
from there you can extend to others.

A while back a friend told me that she realized she needed to take better care of herself. For her, that meant spending less time with other people and more time on her own. She began to feel more grounded and in a much better mental space.

At that same time her mother, with whom she'd had a difficult relationship, became ill and died shortly thereafter. My friend was upset, beating herself up for taking time out for self-care rather than spending time with her mother.

I asked her what it would have been like if she had spent time with her mother. She thought for a while and said, "Not very good, we were always arguing with each other over nothing. She triggered me all the time. That is part of why I realized I needed to take better care of myself, and that meant spending less time with her."

I then asked her how things went in the last two days she had with her mother. She thought again and said, "You know, we got along better than we had in years. I truly felt like we connected and could see each other as individuals. We were peaceful together."

Then she said, "I realize now, in reflecting on it, it was better for me to be away so we could have two good days together. That means more to me, and I'm guessing to her, than a couple months of time where we were at each other's throats."

For me, this is a beautiful illustration of today's theme—that we need to care for ourselves first, and from there extend that care and love to others. If we haven't found a way to love ourselves, it is hard to love others open-heartedly.

Self-Reflection:

Why might extending acceptance and compassion to self and others be useful? Do I find this easy or challenging?

Informal Practice:

Today I will be aware of my own needs and open-heartedly take care of them. Once my needs are met, I will explore opportunities to extend kindness toward others.

Day 62: Win/Lose

Winning is not always important,
for it involves ego. Harmony is important.
Learn to harmonize.
There is no loss in harmony.
There is often loss with a win/lose model.

A friend of mine coaches a youth soccer team. They're a talented team, one of the best in the state. One day I went to a game, and my friend's team was playing a much less skilled team.

Clearly my friend's team was going to win. No one doubted that.

In advance of the game, he talked with his team and let them know he would start players that didn't typically start. He encouraged the kids to play well, but not to play so aggressively that it made the other team look bad. If they were up by two, then everyone would shoot with the weaker foot.

Through this conversation he taught the players on his team how to play well, and show respect for others. He encouraged them to do their best, but not at the cost of embarrassing the other team. He showed them how to harmonize.

My friend showed true leadership that day. Not only did he make a compassionate choice, he also offered a memorable lesson to the young players on his team.

Indeed, his team did win. But it wasn't a complete clobbering. At the end of the game all the kids willingly shook hands, and all faces were smiling.

Self-Reflection:

How often am I more competitive than I need to be? Do I often want to "win" or "be right" in games, conversations or other situations? What would it feel like to harmonize with others around me?

Informal Practice:

Today I will observe my interactions with others. I will intentionally practice being harmonious rather than competitive.

Day 63: Forgiveness

*Forgiveness of self
leads to forgiveness for others.*

One benefit of cultivating acceptance and compassion for self and others is the ability to connect with and extend forgiveness.

As you realize and embrace that you are enough just as you are, you begin releasing past resentments, forgiving yourself for past mistakes, and pardoning others for their mistakes.

Forgiveness is born from acceptance. You may find fault with your past actions, but lean into them with acceptance. You may not like another's past actions, but lean into those with acceptance as well. We are all human beings, we all make mistakes. We all have opportunities for growth.

Practicing compassion automatically connects you to others. As you recognize your own limitations, you can say, "Just like me, this person has experienced pain, anger, frustration, or has made poor decisions." You recognize that all of us are human, and we all have the ability to extend forgiveness.

Self-Reflection:

What memories/concerns/issues from the past can I release today?

Informal Practice:

Today I will get in touch with or send well-wishes to someone from the past for whom I have harbored some ill will or judgment.

Day 64: Control

You can control only your own life.

Personal and spiritual development is a slow and demanding process. It is work that does not end. There is no "getting there." As you gain more insight, the reward is more work. Patience is essential.

You want to meditate better, be more at peace, get a better handle on your life. However, personal and spiritual growth is a natural process, and it can't be rushed. Impatience merely hampers your progress.

Standing in the garden screaming at a seedling to grow faster will not make it bloom sooner. Berating yourself for unskilful behavior likewise will not help your personal growth move faster.

Some things can't be changed. You can't control all of the circumstances around you. However, you can control the way you respond to events.

You can feel defeated by a particular circumstance, or you can choose to view the event as a challenge. You can see it as a test of your ability to maintain tranquility no matter what the occasion. You can see it as an exercise in maintaining patience, courage, and compassion even under duress.

As you find acceptance and tranquility in your own life, you begin releasing the need to control others. As you learn to respond, rather than react, harmonizing becomes easier in all aspects of life.

Self-Reflection:

How often do I try to control the lives of others? Am I successful at it? Does it bring me joy? What would happen if I let go of trying to control the actions of others?

Informal Practice:

Today I will pay attention to moments when I start controlling others (directly or indirectly) and bring that action to a stop. If I want a particular response I will ask for it, and even if I don't get it I will be content.

Day 65: Generosity of Love
Believe in the generosity of love,
for what is given away will come back.

On those grumpy days, when you feel constricted physically and emotionally, have you ever considered the idea that giving something away might open you up?

Offering generosity or altruism, in whatever form makes sense in the moment, may help shift your perspective away from your self-cranky tunnel-vision to the recognition that you have something to offer someone in need.

Altruism can take many forms: offering time or money, opening a door for someone, smiling, or even the simple act of wishing someone well with good intention.

Being generous allows you to view others with greater compassion, as you often find good qualities in people to whom you are kind. Being kind promotes a sense of connection with broader humanity; you begin thinking, "Just like me, this person might appreciate a smile, or a hand with the door."

Being generous helps you appreciate and express gratitude for your own good fortune. Your act of generosity may start a cycle of positive action.

So whether you're feeling cranky or stressed and need a boost, or if you're filled with joy and gratitude; remember that what you give will indeed come back—sometimes in ways you might never have expected or even recognize in the moment.

Self-Reflection:

How often do I offer love freely without expecting something in return?

Informal Practice:

Today I will give the gift of a smile, a gentle touch, a compliment. In turn I will be willing to receive all gifts that come my way.

Day 66: Have Fun!
Have fun! Have fun! Have fun!

It takes intention, motivation, and dedication to build and sustain a compassion meditation practice. It requires looking at and embracing aspects of yourself that you may prefer to suppress, deny, or ignore.

Sometimes it just seems like hard work to keep your mind from drifting off, to practice extending kindness to yourself and others daily.

It isn't easy to practice patience, tolerance, understanding, and acceptance.

But in the long run, cultivating that deeper relationship with yourself is worth the effort.

Meditation can be enjoyable, it isn't always work. In the midst of all that effort and work you need to remember one more thing—to have fun.

Remember to take some time every day—and during your meditation practice—to have fun, have fun, have fun.

Self-Reflection:

How has this practice of acceptance and compassion for self and others changed my view of the world?

Informal Practice:

Today I will move through my day with a smile on my face. I will be proud of the effort I have put into answering self-reflective questions and experimenting with daily informal practices. Today I will look for opportunities to have fun!

EPILOGUE

Congratulations! You've made it through the 66 days of creating a new compassion meditation habit! How do you feel? Great, I bet! Remember, this new habit of daily integrating acceptance and compassion into your life not only benefits you, it benefits everyone around you.

By reading this book, contemplating and writing answers to the self-reflection questions, and taking daily action, you've taken the first steps to incorporating a mindset of acceptance and compassion into everyday life.

If you read through this book in one sitting, I encourage you to go back and take the time to reflect on the questions, and write out the answers. I encourage you to try each of the daily actions.

Some of these inspirations, questions, and actions will be familiar and comfortable to you. They may not take effort, or might not lead you down a growth path.

Some of these inspirations, questions, and actions will be familiar and uncomfortable to you. You might want to skip right over them and not spend any time thinking about or taking action on them. You might want to shove them aside and move on. If that is the case, be kind to yourself. Notice your resistance; work with the questions and actions. If you need to, bookmark the day and come back to it later.

Some of these inspirations, questions, and actions will be brand new ideas to you. Ideas that make perfect sense, but are ideas you'd never really thought of in quite that way.

Embrace all of the concepts—comfortable, un-comfortable, and brand new.

This book was written to help you help yourself grow, change, and consider yourself and your place in the world differently. It was written to offer you tools and techniques for cultivating compassion. I want **all of us** to find peace of mind and resilience, while treating ourselves and each other with acceptance and compassion.

These 66 steps have helped many people find peace of mind, resilience, and become more open-hearted toward others.

You have control over how you live your life.

You have to take action. Integrate these ideas into your life daily. Decide that this is what you want to do.

If I can change my perspective from wanting to jump into a canal of water to teaching courses, coaching, and writing books on compassion meditation, you can change your perspective as well.

We all have the capacity to grow and change.

If you want to overcome stress, depression, or anxiety you can. If you want to lower your blood pressure, settle your mind, and be more creative, you can.

I could have stayed solely with my career as a massage therapist for years to come. I could have helped people one hour at a time. But I wanted to share these insights to help you help yourself. I want you to have access to tools and techniques that empower you to live a healthier, happier, more creative life.

You picked up this book for a reason. It sparked your interest because you are interested in discovering peace of mind and resilience. You are interested in personal growth, or developing a more accepting and compassionate attitude, or overcoming anxiety. Whatever your motivation, put these techniques into action. Not only will you thrive as an individual, you will make a lasting impression on the world.

It is now your turn to shine.

Although these tools and techniques are enough to completely change your life, you may desire more support.

Everyone learns and retains information differently. Some people remember concepts best through reading words, some by recalling images. Now you have access to both.

As a special gift, I want to share with you a FREE companion photo book.

This photo book pairs each of the 66 inspirational themes with photos from my past travels. Perhaps this will be an additional way to help you remember the ideas more vividly.

To receive your free copy visit: .

www.compassionatebalance.com/cultivating-compassion-photo-book/

If you are serious about cultivating compassion in your life, I encourage you to explore my courses or coaching at **www.compassionatebalance.com**. It may be the best investment you make in yourself.

The courses and coaching explore the ideas in this book more deeply. The in-person and online courses create opportunities to discuss ideas with peers in large and small group settings. The concepts are supported by guided meditation. The self-study program offers the same information as the interactive classes, but you proceed at your own pace on your own schedule. The private self-compassion coaching is tailored to support you as you evolve.

If you're interested in guided meditations, you'll find a few I've put together on YouTube: **https://www.youtube.com/compassionatebalance**

Regardless of whether or not you join a class or set up coaching, I want to hear your success stories!

I hope you will send me a note with stories of how you integrated your favorite inspirations, questions, and actions into your life. I would love to hear how you are doing and how your life has changed as a result of ideas sparked by this book.

When you get in touch, please put the book title in the subject heading. You can reach me at **amy@compassionatebalance.com**.

If you enjoyed this book, I would be grateful and honored if you encourage your friends, loved ones, colleagues, or whomever you think might benefit from cultivating compassion, to pick up a copy.

Also, please leave a review on Amazon.com. Your feedback may spark someone else's journey to well-being. Even a brief review would be greatly appreciated. Thanks so much!

Wishing you well,
Amy Pattee Colvin

ABOUT THE AUTHOR

Amy Pattee Colvin first discovered compassion meditation in the mid-1990s via a style called Sum Faht, a blend of Taoism, Buddhism, and Confucianism. Looking for ways to facilitate concepts she learned through Sum Faht meditation in a format that blended with her facilitation style, Amy became a certified facilitator of Stanford University's Compassion Cultivation Training (CCT) program developed at the Center for Compassion and Altruism Research and Education.

By combining her years of Sum Faht practice with elements of the CCT program, she developed a transformative curriculum called Cultivating Compassionate Balance.

She is inspired to help people thrive by sharing tools and techniques that may in turn assist in cultivating self-appreciation, self-acceptance, self-compassion, and compassion for others.

Through the media of her courses, coaching, and this book, Amy offers practical tools and techniques for anyone interested in positive personal growth.

To learn more about Amy, visit:
www.compassionatebalance.com/about-amy/